Man & Messiah
Love & Joy

GREG HAZARD

I am with you always,
to the close of the age.

Matthew 28:20

This work copyright © 2019 Chase Product Concepts

All rights reserved. No part of this work may be reproduced or transmitted in any form or by any means, electronic or mechanical, including photocopying, recording, or by any information storage and retrieval system, without permission in writing from the copyright owner.

Revised Standard Version of the Bible, copyright © 1946, 1952, and 1971 National Council of the Churches of Christ in the United States of America. Used by permission.
All rights reserved.

Scripture references in this work may not appear in their entirety and should not be assumed to be complete. Refer to the Revised Standard Version of the Bible for complete references.

ISBN# 978-0-578-59584-9

Published by Chase Product Concepts
www.cpconcepts.us/MMLJ

Printed in the United States of America

A heartfelt thank you to Kathleen and Corey, Holly and Dominic, Michelle and Paul, and Jordan and Chris. Not just for being great friends and important people in my life, but for reviewing drafts of this book and providing wise input.

A special thank you to my wife, Jodi. Through her love and encouragement she is a true partner and makes possible my ceaseless projects. Most of which never leave our house but all of which consume my time and often invade our kitchen table for days at a stretch.

Table of Contents

Foreword i

Introduction 1

The Collective Text 7

The Reference Text 31

Notes from the Reference Text 57

Foreword

"It's all formative"

As a newly ordained priest, assigned to St. Gabriel Catholic Church in Concord, Ohio, the very first family I had the privilege of registering into the parish community was the Hazard Family. Perhaps it was because they were the first family I would welcome into the parish, or probably because of the wonderful people they are, I have been blessed to have formed a life-long friendship with Greg and his entire family.

As I got to know them, and as I watched parents Pam and Dave form their teen and pre-teen kids into wonderful adults, I would often quip to them that "It's all formative." Indeed, every aspect of life together as a family and community serves to *form* each member. Passing on what matters most requires a clear, focused intentionality to connect faith, life, and family values.

Pam and Dave were actively involved in our parish community and had a special love for faith-sharing groups. Participation in these groups strengthened the connection between the Word and their life. The more they engaged fully in God's work, the more every family outing, every chore, and every meal shaped their family and their children in the Lord and God's Word.

It was, truly, all 'formative'.

The Passion narratives reveal the mind and heart of Jesus Christ. Over and again He embraced the will of the Father and gave His life in loving service to us. Prayerful reflection on the Passion narratives form our own minds and hearts in this pattern and promise of Christ. The more we live the will of the Father, the more we find a fullness of life now and forever.

Most importantly, the Word of God is intended to be formative…to shape our lives, our thoughts and actions in the way we live and what we do. It is truly the wise person that takes God's Word as their Way, Truth, and Life.

Greg has prepared, for all of us, an amazing resource to help us reflect more deeply on God's Word, the hope and promise it contains, and the path to love and joy that it proclaims. The more we take the time to seriously engage in a deeper study and reflection of God's Word, the more we will grow as disciples.

It is a privilege and blessing for me to share these thoughts with you as a foreword to this helpful and valuable resource. It is a testament to the blessing of what happens when a person and his family sets their life and their 'household' on the foundation of the Living Word, Jesus Christ.

May you know the blessings of love and joy that come from knowing the Man and Messiah, Jesus Christ.

Fr. Bob Stec

Introduction

For me, this book was a mission in learning about the Gospels. It began with a curiosity of how the four Gospels told the Passion story differently; using different details, different perspectives, and different accounts of the same events. That curiosity eventually morphed into a personal challenge to combine the Gospel verses into a narrative that was a faithful retelling of the Passion story, that flowed and read like a novel, and that used only text included in the Gospels.

When the varying details from the four Gospels are interlaced with each other, a rich new visual of the story emerges. I chose to use the Revised Standard Version of the Bible for this work. The RSV was published in 1946 by the International Council of Religious Education. With representatives from multiple religious denominations, this committee sought to "embody the best results of modern scholarship as to the meaning of the Scriptures, and express this meaning in English diction which is designed for use in public and private worship, and preserves those qualities which have given to the King James Version a supreme place in English literature."[1]

While each of the four Gospel accounts stands on its own, each offers some detail not contained in the others. Verse selection for this narrative was driven by the desire first, to tell a descriptive and authentic Passion story and, second, to preserve continuity and readability. An appropriate companion to this book is the Bible itself. The verses included here are not always the complete text as found in the RSV and should not be used as such.

It is my hope that this retelling of the Passion is appealing to you, Christian or otherwise, regardless of where on your own personal faith journey you happen to be. Not included in this book is any interpretation of the verses or historical perspective on the Bible. These topics and many others are addressed by scholars, historians, biblical experts, and clergy.

I am none of those things.

This book is simply the product of my own curiosity and I hope that this book may peak your own interest and stir you to pull a Bible off the shelf, to draw your own conclusions, and to progress along whatever faith path you are traveling.

----

[1] Excerpt taken from the Preface to the Revised Standard Version (1971, on the occasion of the second edition of the New Testament)

There are two sets of text in this book. The first is the Collective Text. This is a single narrative of the passion story weaving together descriptive elements from all four Gospels. The words contained in the Collective Text are straight from the Gospels, save for a few exceptions. On certain occasions, it was necessary to add a proper name, preposition, noun, or other word in order to make the Collective text read smoothly. Great care was taken to keep these additions to an absolute minimum and to ensure that they were used in a way that only clarified the reading and did not change its meaning, context, or impact. In the Collective Text, these additional words are *italicized* to indicate that they are not from the biblical text. No liberty was taken to embellish any part of the story beyond what appears in one of the Gospels.

After the Collective Text comes the Reference Text. This text reads exactly the same as the Collective, however, the Reference text has two additional elements.

1. Color Coded: In the Reference text the words appear in one of five colors. You will see blue, green, red, orange, and black. The key to this color code is across the top of each left-hand page. Here you will see the four Gospel names of Matthew, Mark, Luke, and John, each in their own color. The corresponding color of the text indicates in which Gospel it can be found. Words that have been added for clarity and flow are in black.

2. Chapter & Verse Reference: Throughout the Reference Text you will see chapter and verse references in the standard form of [chapter number ":" verse number.] This reference, combined with the text color,

can be used to find that passage in the Revised Standard Version of the Bible. Where only a portion of a verse has been used, "…" is put in place of the omitted portion.

Each paragraph is numbered to allow easy reference between the two sets of text.

Example 1

Collective Text

When Jesus had spoken these words, he went forth with his disciples, as was his custom, to the Mount of Olives; across the Kidron valley, where there was a garden called Gethsem'ane. He said to his disciples, "Sit here, while I pray."

Reference Text

Matthew | Mark | Luke | John
18:1 When Jesus had spoken these words, he went forth with his disciples… 22:39 …as was his custom, to the Mount of Olives;… 18:1 …across the Kidron valley, where there was a garden… 26:36 …called Gethsem'ane… 14:32 …he said to his disciples, "Sit here, while I pray."

Example 2

Collective Text

Jesus answered *again*, "I told you that I am he; so, if you seek me, let these men go." Then they came up and laid hands on Jesus and seized him. Simon Peter drew his sword and struck the slave of the high priest, *whose* name was Malchus, and cut off his ear. But Jesus said, "No more of this!" and he touched his ear and healed him.

Reference Text

Matthew | Mark | Luke | John
18:8 Jesus answered... *again* ..."I told you that I am he; so, if you seek me, let these men go." 26:50 ...then they came up and laid hands on Jesus and seized him. 18:10 ...Simon Peter... 14:47 ...drew his sword, and struck the slave of the high priest,... *whose* 18:10 ...name was Malchus, 14:47 ...and cut off his ear. 22:51 But Jesus said, "No more of this!" And he touched his ear and healed him.

Collective Text

----

1   Now on the first day of Unleavened Bread the disciples came to Jesus, saying, "Where will you have us prepare for you to eat the passover?" He sent two of his disciples and said to them, "Go into the city and a man carrying a jar of water will meet you, follow him into the house which he enters and tell the householder, 'The Teacher says to you, where is the guest room where I am to eat the passover with my disciples?' He will show you a large upper room furnished; there make ready." And they went, and found it as he had told them; and they prepared the passover.

2   Now before the feast of the Passover, when Jesus knew that his hour had come to depart out of this world to the Father, having loved his own who were in the world, he loved them to the end. And during supper,

when the devil had already put it into the heart of Judas Iscariot to betray him, Jesus, knowing that the Father had given all things into his hands, and that he had come from God and was going to God, rose from supper, laid aside his garments, and girded himself with a towel. Then he poured water into a basin, and began to wash the disciples' feet, and to wipe them with the towel with which he was girded. He came to Simon Peter; and Peter said to him, "Lord, do you wash my feet?" Jesus answered him, "What I am doing you do not know now, but afterward you will understand."

3   When he had washed their feet, taken his garments, and resumed his place, he said to them, "Do you know what I have done to you? You call me Teacher and Lord; and you are right, for so I am. If I then, your Lord and Teacher, have washed your feet, you also ought to wash one another's feet. For I have given you an example, that you also should do as I have done to you. Truly, truly, I say to you, a servant is not greater than his master; nor is he who is sent greater than he who sent him. If you know these things, blessed are you if you do them."

4   *Jesus continued* "I have earnestly desired to eat this passover with you before I suffer; for I tell you I shall not eat it until it is fulfilled in the kingdom of God." He took bread, and when he had given thanks he broke it and gave it to them, saying, "This is my body which is given for you. Do this in remembrance of me." And he took a cup, and when he had given thanks he gave it to them, saying, "Drink of it, all of you; for this is my blood of the covenant, which is poured out for many for the

forgiveness of sins. I tell you I shall not drink again of this fruit of the vine until that day when I drink it new with you in my Father's kingdom."

5   And as they were at *the* table eating, Jesus *continued*, "Truly, I say to you, one of you will betray me, one who is eating with me." The disciples looked at one another, uncertain of whom he spoke. They began to be sorrowful, and to say to him one after another, "Is it I?" Jesus answered, "It is he to whom I shall give this morsel when I have dipped it." So when *Jesus* had dipped the morsel, he gave it to Judas. Jesus said to him, "What you are going to do, do quickly." So, after receiving the morsel, *Judas* immediately went out; it was night.

6   When *Judas* had gone out, Jesus said, "As I said to the Jews so now I say to you, 'Where I am going you cannot come.' A new commandment I give to you, that you love one another; even as I have loved you, by this all men will know that you are my disciples, if you have love for one another."

7   Simon Peter said to him, "Lord, where are you going?" Jesus answered, "Where I am going you cannot follow me now; but you shall follow afterward. You will all fall away; for it is written, 'I will strike the shepherd, and the sheep will be scattered.' But after I am raised up, I will go before you to Galilee." Peter said to him, "Even though they all fall away, I will not." Jesus *replied*, "Truly, I say to you, this very night, before the cock crows twice, you will deny me three times." But he said vehemently, "If I must die with you, I will not deny you." And they all said the same.

8   When Jesus had spoken these words, he went

forth with his disciples, as was his custom, to the Mount of Olives; across the Kidron valley, where there was a garden called Gethsem′ane. He said to his disciples, "Sit here, while I pray." He took with him Peter and the two sons of Zeb′edee, James and John, and began to be greatly distressed and troubled. He said to them "My soul is very sorrowful, even to death; remain here, and watch with me. Pray that you may not enter into temptation." He withdrew from them about a stone's throw, and knelt down and prayed that, if it were possible, the hour might pass from him. And he said, "Abba, Father, all things are possible to thee; remove this cup from me; yet not what I will, but what thou *will*." Then an angel from heaven appeared to him and gave him strength. In his anguish he prayed more earnestly, and his sweat became like great drops of blood falling down on the ground.

9   When he rose from prayer, he came to the disciples and found them sleeping. He said to Peter, "Simon, are you asleep? Could you not watch with me one hour? Watch and pray that you may not enter into temptation; the spirit indeed is willing, but the flesh is weak." Again, for the second time, he went away and prayed, "My Father, if this cannot pass unless I drink it, thy will be done." Again he came and found them sleeping, for their eyes were heavy. So, leaving them again, he went away and prayed for the third time, saying the same words. Then he came to the disciples and said to them, "Are you still sleeping and taking your rest? It is enough; the hour has come; the Son of man is betrayed into the hands of sinners. Rise, let us be going; see, my betrayer is at hand."

10 Now Judas, who betrayed him, also knew the place; for Jesus often met there with his disciples. So Judas, procuring a band of soldiers and some officers from the chief priests and the Pharisees, went there with lanterns and torches and weapons. Now the betrayer had given them a sign, saying, "The one I shall kiss is the man; seize him and lead him away under guard."

11 While *Jesus* was still speaking, Judas came. He drew near to Jesus to kiss him. Jesus said to him, "Judas, would you betray the Son of man with a kiss?" Jesus, knowing all that was to befall him, came forward and said to them, "Whom do you seek?" They answered, "Jesus of Nazareth." Jesus said, "I am he." When he said *this* they drew back. Again he asked, "Whom do you seek?" And they said, "Jesus of Nazareth." Jesus answered *again*, "I told you that I am he; so, if you seek me, let these men go." Then they came up and laid hands on Jesus and seized him. Simon Peter drew his sword, and struck the slave of the high priest, *whose* name was Malchus, and cut off his ear. But Jesus said, "No more of this!" and he touched his ear and healed him. Jesus said to *Peter,* "Put your sword back into its place; for all who take the sword will perish by the sword. Do you think that I cannot appeal to my Father, and he will at once send me more than twelve legions of angels? But how then should the scriptures be fulfilled?" At that hour Jesus said to the crowds, "Have you come out as against a robber, with swords and clubs to capture me? Day after day I was with you in the temple teaching, and you did not seize me. But all this has taken place, that the scriptures of the prophets might be fulfilled."

12 Then those who had seized Jesus *took* him to Ca`iaphas the high priest, where the scribes and the elders had gathered. Peter followed Jesus and so did another disciple. As this disciple was known to the high priest, he entered the court of the high priest along with Jesus while Peter stood outside at the door. So the other disciple went out and spoke to the maid who kept the door and brought Peter in. The maid said to Peter, "You were with Jesus the Galilean." But he denied it before them all, saying, "I do not know what you mean." Now the servants and officers had made a charcoal fire, because it was cold, and they were standing and warming themselves; Peter also was with them, standing and warming himself.

13 First they led *Jesus* to Annas; for he was the father-in-law of Caiaphas, who was high priest that year. It was Ca'iaphas who had given counsel to the Jews that it was expedient that one man should die for the people. Now the chief priests and the whole council sought false testimony against Jesus that they might put him to death, but they found none. At last two came forward and said, "We heard him say, 'I will destroy this temple that is made with hands, and in three days I will build another, not made with hands.'" The high priest stood up and said, "Have you no answer to make? What is it that these men testify against you?" But *Jesus* was silent and made no answer. Again the high priest asked him, "Are you the Christ, the Son of the Blessed?" Jesus said to him, "You have said so. But I tell you, hereafter you will see the Son of man seated at the right hand of Power, and coming on the clouds of heaven." Then the high priest tore his robes,

and said, "Why do we still need witnesses? You have heard his blasphemy. What is your decision?" They answered, "He deserves death." And some began to spit on him, and to cover his face, and to strike him, saying to him, "Prophesy!" And the guards received him with blows.

14   The high priest then questioned Jesus about his disciples and his teaching. Jesus answered him, "I have spoken openly to the world; I have always taught in synagogues and in the temple, where all Jews come together; I have said nothing secretly. Why do you ask me? Ask those who have heard me, they know what I said." When he had said this, one of the officers standing by struck Jesus with his hand, saying, "Is that how you answer the high priest?" Jesus *replied*, "If I have spoken wrongly, bear witness to the wrong; but if I have spoken rightly, why do you strike me?" Annas then sent him bound to Ca'iaphas the high priest.

15   *As* Peter was standing and warming himself, they said to him, "Are not you also one of his disciples?" He denied it and said, "I am not." After a little while one of the servants of the high priest, a kinsman of the man whose ear Peter had cut off, asked, "Certainly you are also one of them, for your accent betrays you." Then he began to invoke a curse on himself and to swear, "I do not know the man." And immediately, while he was still speaking, the cock crowed. The Lord turned and looked at Peter and Peter remembered how he had said to him, "Before the cock crows today, you will deny me three times." And *Peter* went out and wept bitterly.

16   Now the men who were holding Jesus mocked

him and beat him; they also blindfolded him and asked him, "Prophesy! Who is it that struck you?" And they spoke many other words against him, reviling him.

17 When day came, the assembly of the elders of the people gathered together, both chief priests and scribes, and they led him away to their council. They said *to Jesus*, "If you are the Christ, tell us." But he said to them, "If I tell you, you will not believe; and if I ask you, you will not answer. But from now on the Son of man shall be seated at the right hand of the power of God." And they all said, "Are you the Son of God, then?" *Jesus replied*, "You say that I am." And they said, "What further testimony do we need? We have heard it ourselves from his own lips."

18 When Judas, his betrayer, saw that he was condemned, he repented and brought back the thirty pieces of silver to the chief priests and the elders, saying, "I have sinned in betraying innocent blood." They said, "What is that to us? See to it yourself." And throwing down the pieces of silver in the temple, he departed and he went and hanged himself. But the chief priests, taking the pieces of silver, said, "It is not lawful to put them into the treasury since they are blood money." So they took counsel, and bought with them the potter's field to bury strangers in. Therefore that field has been called the Field of Blood to this day. Then was fulfilled what had been spoken by the prophet Jeremiah, saying, "And they took the thirty pieces of silver, the price of him on whom a price had been set by some of the sons of Israel, and they gave them for the potter's field, as the Lord directed me."

19 Then they led Jesus from the house of Ca′iaphas

to the praetorium and delivered him to Pilate. It was early *and* the chief priests themselves did not enter the praetorium so that they might not be defiled, but might eat the passover. So Pilate went out to them and said, "What accusation do you bring against this man?" They answered him, "If this man were not an evildoer, we would not have handed him over." Pilate said to them, "Take him yourselves and judge him by your own law." The Jews said, "It is not lawful for us to put any man to death." This was to fulfill the word which Jesus had spoken to show by what death he was to die.

20   Pilate entered the praetorium and called Jesus. Now Jesus stood before the governor; and the governor asked him, "Are you the King of the Jews?", Jesus said "Do you say this of your own accord, or did others say it to you about me?" Pilate answered, "Am I a Jew? Your own nation and the chief priests have handed you over to me; what have you done?" Jesus answered, "My kingship is not of this world; if my kingship were of this world, my servants would fight, that I might not be handed over to the Jews; but my kingship is not from the world." Pilate said to him, "So you are a king?" Jesus answered, "You say that I am a king. For this I was born, and for this I have come into the world, to bear witness to the truth. Every one who is of the truth hears my voice." Pilate said to him, "What is truth? Do you not hear how many things they testify against you?" But Jesus made no further answer.

21   After this Pilate went out to the Jews again and said to the chief priests and the multitudes, "I find no crime in this man." But they were urgent, saying, "He

stirs up the people, teaching throughout all Judea, from Galilee even to this place." When Pilate heard this, he asked whether the man was a Galilean. And when he learned that he belonged to Herod's jurisdiction, he sent him over to Herod, who was himself in Jerusalem at that time. When Herod saw Jesus, he was very glad for he had long desired to see him and he was hoping to see some sign done by him. So he questioned him at some length. But *Jesus* made no answer. The chief priests and the scribes stood by, vehemently accusing him. And Herod with his soldiers treated him with contempt and mocked him. Then, arraying him in gorgeous apparel, he sent him back to Pilate. Herod and Pilate became friends with each other that very day, for before this they had been at enmity with each other.

22   Now at the Passover feast the governor was accustomed to release for the crowd any one prisoner whom they wanted. Among the rebels in prison, who had committed murder in the insurrection, there was a man called Barab'bas. Pilate then called together the chief priests and the rulers and the people, and said to them, "You brought me this man as one who was perverting the people; and after examining him before you, behold, I did not find this man guilty of any of your charges against him; neither did Herod, for he sent him back to us. Behold, nothing deserving death has been done by him." But they all cried out together, "Away with this man, and release to us Barab'bas". Pilate again said to them, "Then what shall I do with the man whom you call the King of the Jews?" And they cried out again, "Crucify him." Pilate said, "Why, what evil has he done?" But they

shouted all the more, "Crucify him."

23   Pilate said to them, "Take him yourselves and crucify him, for I find no crime in him." The Jews answered him, "We have a law, and by that law he ought to die, because he has made himself the Son of God." When Pilate heard these words, he was the more afraid; he entered the praetorium again and said to Jesus, "Where are you from?" But Jesus gave no answer. Pilate therefore said to him, "You will not speak to me? Do you not know that I have power to release you, and power to crucify you?" Jesus answered, "You would have no power over me unless it had been given you from above; therefore he who delivered me to you has the greater sin."

24   Upon this Pilate sought to release him, but the Jews cried out, "If you release this man, you are not Caesar's friend; every one who makes himself a king sets himself against Caesar." When Pilate heard these words, he brought Jesus out and sat down on the judgment seat at a place called The Pavement; and in Hebrew, Gab′batha. While he was sitting on the judgment seat his wife sent word to him, "Have nothing to do with that righteous man, for I have suffered much over him today in a dream."

25   Now it was the day of Preparation of the Passover; it was about the sixth hour. He said to the Jews, "Behold your King!" They cried out, "Away with him, away with him, crucify him!" So when Pilate saw that he was gaining nothing, but rather that a riot was beginning, he took water and washed his hands before the crowd, saying, "I am innocent of this man's blood; see to it

yourselves." And all the people answered, "His blood be on us and on our children!" Then he released for them Barab′bas, and having scourged Jesus, delivered him to be crucified.

26   The soldiers led him away into the praetorium, and they gathered the whole battalion before him. They stripped him and put a scarlet robe upon him and plaiting a crown of thorns, they put it on his head and put a reed in his right hand. Kneeling before him they mocked him, saying, "Hail, King of the Jews!" And they began to salute him. They struck his head with a reed, and spat upon him, and they knelt down in homage to him. When they had mocked him, they stripped him of the robe, put his own clothes on him, and led him away to crucify him.

27   They took Jesus, and he went out, bearing his own cross. And as they led him away they seized Simon of Cyre′ne, the father of Alexander and Rufus, to carry his cross. And there followed him a great multitude of the people, and of women who bewailed and lamented him. But Jesus, turning to them, said, "Daughters of Jerusalem, do not weep for me, but weep for yourselves and for your children. For behold, the days are coming when they will say, 'Blessed are the barren, and the wombs that never bore, and the breasts that never gave suck!' Then they will begin to say to the mountains, 'Fall on us'; and to the hills, 'Cover us.' For if they do this when the wood is green, what will happen when it is dry?"

28   Two others also, who were criminals, were led away to be put to death with *Jesus*. And when they came to the place called Gol′gotha (which, in Hebrew means

the place of a skull), they crucified him, and the criminals, one on the right and one on the left. And Jesus said, "Father, forgive them; for they know not what they do." They offered him wine mingled with myrrh; but he did not take it. Pilate wrote a title and put it on the cross; it read, "Jesus of Nazareth, the King of the Jews." Many of the Jews read this title, for the place where Jesus was crucified was near the city; and it was written in Hebrew, in Latin, and in Greek. The chief priests of the Jews then said to Pilate, "Do not write, 'The King of the Jews,' but, 'This man said, I am King of the Jews.'" Pilate answered, "What I have written I have written."

29 The soldiers took his garments and made four parts, one for each soldier; also his tunic. But the tunic was without seam, woven from top to bottom; so they said to one another, "Let us not tear it, but cast lots for it to see whose it shall be." This was to fulfill the scripture, "They parted my garments among them, and for my clothing they cast lots."

30 The people stood by watching but the rulers scoffed at him, saying, "He saved others; let him save himself, if he is the Christ of God, his Chosen One! You who would destroy the temple and build it in three days, save yourself! If you are the Son of God, come down from the cross." So also the chief priests, with the scribes and elders, mocked him, saying, "He saved others; he cannot save himself. Let the Christ, the King of Israel, come down now from the cross, that we may see and believe."

31 One of the criminals who were hanged railed at him, saying, "Are you not the Christ? Save yourself and

us!" But the other rebuked him, saying, "Do you not fear God, since you are under the same sentence of condemnation? And we indeed justly; for we are receiving the due reward of our deeds; but this man has done nothing wrong." And he *continued*, "Jesus, remember me when you come into your kingdom." *Jesus* said to him, "Truly, I say to you, today you will be with me in Paradise."

32   Standing by the cross of Jesus were his mother, and his mother's sister, Mary the wife of Clopas, and Mary Mag′dalene. When Jesus saw his mother and *John*, the disciple whom he loved, standing near he said to his mother, "Woman, behold, your son!" Then he said to the disciple, "Behold, your mother!" And from that hour the disciple took her to his own home.

33   At the ninth hour while the sun's light failed, Jesus cried with a loud voice, "E′lo-i, E′lo-i, la′ma sabachtha′ni?" which means, "My God, my God, why hast thou forsaken me?" And some of the bystanders hearing it said, "Behold, he is calling Eli′jah." After this, Jesus, knowing that all was now finished, said "I thirst." A bowl full of vinegar stood there; so they put a sponge full of the vinegar on hyssop and held it to his mouth. When Jesus had received the vinegar, he said, "It is finished" Having said this he bowed his head, breathed his last, and gave up his spirit.

---

34   And behold, the curtain of the temple was torn in two, from top to bottom; and the earth shook, and the rocks were split; the tombs also were opened, and many bodies of the saints who had fallen asleep were raised. When the centurion and those who were with him, keeping watch over Jesus, saw the earthquake and what took place, they were filled with awe, and said, "Truly this was the Son of God!" There were also women looking on from afar, among whom were Mary Mag'dalene, and Mary the mother of James the younger and of Joses, and Salo'me who, when he was in Galilee, followed him and ministered to him; and also many other women who came up with him to Jerusalem.

35   Since it was the day of Preparation, in order to prevent the bodies from remaining on the cross on the sabbath (for that sabbath was a high day), the Jews asked Pilate that their legs might be broken, and that they might be taken away. So the soldiers came and broke the legs of the first, and of the other who had been crucified with him; but when they came to Jesus and saw that he was already dead, they did not break his legs. But one of the soldiers pierced his side with a spear, and at once there came out blood and water. He who saw it has borne witness. His testimony is true, and he knows that he tells the truth, that you also may believe. For these things took place that the scripture might be fulfilled, "Not a bone of him shall be broken." And again another scripture says, "They shall look on him whom they have pierced."

36   When it was evening Joseph of Arimathe'a, a respected member of the council, who was also himself

looking for the kingdom of God, took courage and went to Pilate and asked for the body of Jesus. Pilate wondered if he were already dead; and summoning the centurion, he asked him whether he was already dead. When he learned from the centurion that he was dead, *Pilot* granted the body to Joseph. So he came and took away his body. Nicode′mus also, who had at first come to him by night, came bringing a mixture of myrrh and aloes, about a hundred pounds' weight. They took the body of Jesus and bound it in linen cloths with the spices, as is the burial custom of the Jews. Now in the place where he was crucified there was a garden, and in the garden a new rock-hewn tomb where no one had ever been laid. So because of the Jewish day of Preparation, as the tomb was close at hand, they laid Jesus there.

37   The women who had come with him from Galilee followed, and saw the tomb, and how his body was laid; then they returned, and prepared spices and ointments. On the Sabbath they rested according to the commandment.

38   *The* next day, that is, after the day of Preparation, the chief priests and the Pharisees gathered before Pilate and said, "Sir, we remember how that imposter said, while he was still alive, 'After three days I will rise again.' Therefore order the sepulcher to be made secure until the third day, lest his disciples go and steal him away, and tell the people, 'He has risen from the dead,' and the last fraud will be worse than the first." Pilate said to them, "You have a guard of soldiers. Go, make it as secure as you can." So they went and made the sepulcher secure by sealing the stone and setting a guard.

39   And when the sabbath was past, toward the dawn of the first day of the week, Mary Mag'dalene, and Mary the mother of James, and Salo'me, bought spices, so that they might go and anoint him. They were saying to one another, "Who will roll away the stone for us from the door of the tomb?" And behold, there was a great earthquake; for an angel of the Lord descended from heaven and came, rolled back the stone, and sat upon it. His appearance was like lightning, and his raiment white as snow. For fear of him the guards trembled and became like dead men. But when *the women* went in they did not find the body. While they were perplexed about this, the angel said to *them*, "Why do you seek the living among the dead? Remember how he told you, while he was still in Galilee, that the Son of man must be delivered into the hands of sinful men, and be crucified, and on the third day rise." And they remembered his words. *The angel continued.* "Do not be afraid. He is not here; for he has risen, as he said. Go quickly. Tell his disciples and Peter that he is going before you to Galilee; there you will see him." So they departed quickly from the tomb with fear and great joy, and ran to tell his disciples.

40   Peter then came out with the other disciple, the one whom Jesus loved, and they went toward the tomb. They both ran, but the other disciple outran Peter and reached the tomb first; and stooping to look in, he saw the linen cloths lying there, but he did not go in. Then Peter came, following him, and went into the tomb. He saw the linen cloths lying and the napkin, which had been on his head, not lying with the linen cloths but rolled up in a place by itself. Then the other disciple, who reached

the tomb first, also went in and he saw and believed; for as yet they did not know the scripture that he must rise from the dead. Then the disciples went back to their homes.

41   *Now* Mary *Mag'dalene* stood weeping outside the tomb, and as she wept she stooped to look into the tomb. *The* angels in white, sitting where the body of Jesus had lain, one at the head and one at the feet, said to her, "Woman, why are you weeping?" She said to them, "Because they have taken away my Lord, and I do not know where they have laid him." Saying this, she turned round and saw Jesus standing, but she did not know that it was Jesus. Jesus said to her, "Woman, why are you weeping? Whom do you seek?" Supposing him to be the gardener, she said to him, "Sir, if you have carried him away, tell me where you have laid him and I will take him away." Jesus said to her, "Mary." She turned and said to him in Hebrew, "Rab-bo'ni!" (which means Teacher). Jesus said to her, "Do not hold me, for I have not yet ascended to the Father; but go to my brethren and say to them, I am ascending to my Father and your Father, to my God and your God." Mary went and said to the disciples, "I have seen the Lord"; and she told them that he had said these things to her.

42   Some of the guard went into the city and told the chief priests all that had taken place. And when they had assembled with the elders and taken counsel, they gave a sum of money to the soldiers and said, "Tell people, 'His disciples came by night and stole him away while we were asleep.' And if this comes to the governor's ears, we will satisfy him and keep you out of trouble." So they

took the money and did as they were directed; and this story has been spread among the Jews to this day.

43   That very day two of *Jesus' followers* were going to a village named Emma'us, about seven miles from Jerusalem, and *talked* with each other about all these things that had happened. While they were talking and discussing together, Jesus himself drew near and went with them. But their eyes were kept from recognizing him. And he said to them, "What is this conversation which you are holding with each other as you walk?" And they stood still, looking sad.

44   Then one of them, named Cle'opas, answered him, "Are you the only visitor to Jerusalem who does not know the things that have happened there in these days?" And he said to them, "What things?" *They replied*, "Concerning Jesus of Nazareth, who was a prophet mighty in deed and word before God and all the people. And how our chief priests and rulers delivered him up to be condemned to death and crucified him. But we had hoped that he was the one to redeem Israel. Yes, and besides all this, it is now the third day since this happened. Moreover, some women of our company amazed us. They were at the tomb early in the morning and did not find his body; and they came back saying that they had even seen a vision of angels who said that he was alive. Some of those who were with us went to the tomb and found it just as the women had said; but him they did not see."

45   He said to them, "O foolish men, and slow of heart to believe all that the prophets have spoken! Was it not necessary that the Christ should suffer these things

and enter into his glory?" And beginning with Moses and all the prophets, he interpreted to them, in all the scriptures, the things concerning himself.

46   So they drew near to the village to which they were going. He appeared to be going further but they constrained him saying, "Stay with us, for it is toward evening and the day is now far spent." So he went in to stay with them. When he was at table with them, he took the bread, blessed and broke it, and gave it to them. Their eyes were opened and *as* they recognized him, he vanished out of their sight. They said to each other, "Did not our hearts burn within us while he talked to us on the road, while he opened, to us, the scriptures?"

47   *The two* rose that same hour and returned to Jerusalem; and they found the eleven gathered together. *Even with* the doors being shut for fear of the Jews, Jesus came and stood among them and said to them, "Peace be with you." When he had said this, he showed them his hands and his side. Then the disciples were glad when they saw the Lord. Jesus said to them again, "Peace be with you. As the Father has sent me, even so I send you." And when he had said this, he breathed on them, and said to them, "Receive the Holy Spirit. If you forgive the sins of any, they are forgiven; if you retain the sins of any, they are retained."

48   Now Thomas, one of the twelve, called the Twin, was not with them when Jesus came. So the other disciples told him, "We have seen the Lord." But he said to them, "Unless I see in his hands the print of the nails, and place my finger in the mark of the nails, and place my hand in his side, I will not believe."

49   Eight days later, his disciples were again in the house and Thomas was with them. The doors were shut, but Jesus came and stood among them, and said, "Peace be with you." Then he said to Thomas, "Put your finger here, and see my hands; and put out your hand, and place it in my side; do not be faithless, but believing." Thomas answered him, "My Lord and my God!" Jesus said to him, "Have you believed because you have seen me? Blessed are those who have not seen and yet believe."

50   After this Jesus revealed himself again to the disciples by the Sea of Tibe′ri-as; and he revealed himself in this way. Simon Peter, Thomas called the Twin, Nathan′a-el of Cana in Galilee, the sons of Zeb′edee, and two others of his disciples were together. Simon Peter said to them, "I am going fishing." They said to him, "We will go with you." They went out and got into the boat; but that night they caught nothing.

51   Just as day was breaking, Jesus stood on the beach; yet the disciples did not know that it was Jesus. Jesus said to them, "Children, have you any fish?" They answered him, "No." He said to them, "Cast the net on the right side of the boat, and you will find some." So they cast it, and now they were not able to haul it in, for the quantity of fish. That disciple whom Jesus loved said to Peter, "It is the Lord!" When Simon Peter heard that it was the Lord, he put on his clothes, for he was stripped for work, and sprang into the sea. But the other disciples came in the boat, dragging the net full of fish, for they were not far from the land, but about a hundred yards off.

52   When they got out on land, they saw a charcoal

fire there, with fish lying on it, and bread. Jesus said to them, "Bring some of the fish that you have just caught." So Simon Peter went aboard and hauled the net ashore, full of large fish, a hundred and fifty-three of them; and although there were so many, the net was not torn. Jesus said to them, "Come and have breakfast." Now none of the disciples dared ask him, "Who are you?" They knew it was the Lord. Jesus came and took the bread and gave it to them, and so with the fish. This was now the third time that Jesus was revealed to the disciples after he was raised from the dead.

53   When they had finished breakfast, Jesus said to Simon Peter, "Simon, son of John, do you love me more than these?" He said to him, "Yes, Lord; you know that I love you." *Jesus* said, "Feed my lambs." A second time he said to *Peter*, "Simon, son of John, do you love me?" He said to him, "Yes, Lord; you know that I love you." He said to him, "Tend my sheep." *Jesus* said the third time, "Simon, son of John, do you love me?" Peter was grieved because he said to him the third time, "Do you love me?" And he said to him, "Lord, you know everything; you know that I love you." Jesus said to him, "Feed my sheep. Truly, truly, I say to you, when you were young, you girded yourself and walked where you would; but when you are old, you will stretch out your hands, and another will gird you and carry you where you do not wish to go." (This he said to show by what death he was to glorify God.)

54   *Then* he said to them, "Go into all the world and preach the gospel to the whole creation. He who believes and is baptized will be saved; but he who does not believe

will be condemned. And these signs will accompany those who believe: in my name they will cast out demons; they will speak in new tongues; they will pick up serpents, and if they drink any deadly thing, it will not hurt them; they will lay their hands on the sick, and they will recover." And after this he said, "Follow me."

55 Then he led them out as far as Bethany, and lifting up his hands he blessed them, *saying*, "All authority in heaven and on earth has been given to me. Go therefore and make disciples of all nations, baptizing them in the name of the Father and of the Son and of the Holy Spirit, teaching them to observe all that I have commanded you.

56 "I am with you always, to the close of the age."

57 While he blessed them he parted from them, was carried up into heaven, and sat down at the right hand of God.

Reference Text

---

1   26:17 Now on the first day of Unleavened Bread the disciples came to Jesus, saying, "Where will you have us prepare for you to eat the passover?" 14:13 …He sent two of his disciples, and said to them, "Go into the city, and a man carrying a jar of water will meet you... 22:10 …follow him into the house which he enters, 22:11 and tell the householder, 'The Teacher says to you, Where is the guest room, where I am to eat the passover with my disciples?' 22:12 …he will show you a large upper room furnished; there make ready." 22:13 And they went, and found it as he had told them; and they prepared the passover.

2   13:1 Now before the feast of the Passover, when Jesus knew that his hour had come to depart out of this world to the Father, having loved his own who were in

the world, he loved them to the end. 13:2 And during supper, when the devil had already put it into the heart of Judas Iscariot...to betray him, 13:3 Jesus, knowing that the Father had given all things into his hands, and that he had come from God and was going to God, 13:4 rose from supper, laid aside his garments, and girded himself with a towel. 13:5 Then he poured water into a basin, and began to wash the disciples' feet, and to wipe them with the towel with which he was girded. 13:6 He came to Simon Peter; and Peter said to him, "Lord, do you wash my feet?" 13:7 Jesus answered him, "What I am doing you do not know now, but afterward you will understand."

3   13:12 When he had washed their feet, ...taken his garments, and resumed his place, he said to them, "Do you know what I have done to you? 13:13 You call me Teacher and Lord; and you are right, for so I am. 13:14 If I then, your Lord and Teacher, have washed your feet, you also ought to wash one another's feet. 13:15 For I have given you an example, that you also should do as I have done to you. 13:16 Truly, truly, I say to you, a servant is not greater than his master; nor is he who is sent greater than he who sent him. 13:17 If you know these things, blessed are you if you do them."

4   *Jesus continued* 22:15 ..."I have earnestly desired to eat this passover with you before I suffer; 22:16 for I tell you I shall not eat it until it is fulfilled in the kingdom of God." 22:19 ...he took bread, and when he had given thanks he broke it and gave it to them, saying, "This is my body which is given for you. Do this in remembrance of me." 26:27 And he took a cup, and when he had given

thanks he gave it to them, saying, "Drink of it, all of you; 26:28 for this is my blood of the covenant, which is poured out for many for the forgiveness of sins. 26:29 I tell you I shall not drink again of this fruit of the vine until that day when I drink it new with you in my Father's kingdom."

5   14:18 And as they were at...*the*...table eating, Jesus... *continued*, ..."Truly, I say to you, one of you will betray me, one who is eating with me." 13:22 The disciples looked at one another, uncertain of whom he spoke. 14:19 They began to be sorrowful, and to say to him one after another, "Is it I?" 13:26 Jesus answered, "It is he to whom I shall give this morsel when I have dipped it." So when... *Jesus* ...had dipped the morsel, he gave it to Judas.... 13:27 ...Jesus said to him, "What you are going to do, do quickly." 13:30 So, after receiving the morsel,... *Judas* ...immediately went out; it was night.

6   13:31 When... *Judas* ...had gone out, Jesus said..., 13:33 "...As I said to the Jews so now I say to you, 'Where I am going you cannot come.' 13:34 A new commandment I give to you, that you love one another; even as I have loved you,... 13:35 By this all men will know that you are my disciples, if you have love for one another."

7   13:36 Simon Peter said to him, "Lord, where are you going?" Jesus answered, "Where I am going you cannot follow me now; but you shall follow afterward." 14:27 ..."You will all fall away; for it is written, 'I will strike the shepherd, and the sheep will be scattered.' 14:28 But after I am raised up, I will go before you to Galilee." 14:29 Peter said to him, "Even though they all fall away, I

Matthew | Mark | Luke | John

will not." 14:30 …Jesus… ***replied***, …"Truly, I say to you, this very night, before the cock crows twice, you will deny me three times." 14:31 But he said vehemently, "If I must die with you, I will not deny you." And they all said the same.

8   N1 18:1 When Jesus had spoken these words, he went forth with his disciples… 22:39 …as was his custom, to the Mount of Olives;… 18:1 …across the Kidron valley, where there was a garden… 26:36 …called Gethsem'ane… 14:32 …he said to his disciples, "Sit here, while I pray." 14:33 He took with him Peter and… 26:37 …the two sons of Zeb'edee… 14:33 …James and John, and began to be greatly distressed and troubled. 14:34 He said to them… 26:38 …"My soul is very sorrowful, even to death; remain here, and watch with me." 22:40 …"Pray that you may not enter into temptation." 22:41 …he withdrew from them about a stone's throw, and knelt down and prayed 14:35 …that, if it were possible, the hour might pass from him. 14:36 And he said, "Abba, Father, all things are possible to thee; remove this cup from me; yet not what I will, but what thou… ***will***." N2 [22:43 Then an angel from heaven appeared to him and gave him strength. 22:44 In his anguish he prayed more earnestly, and his sweat became like great drops of blood falling down on the ground.]

9   22:45 …when he rose from prayer, he came to the disciples and found them sleeping… 14:37 …he said to Peter, "Simon, are you asleep?... 26:40 …could you not watch with me one hour? 26:41 Watch and pray that you

may not enter into temptation; the spirit indeed is willing, but the flesh is weak." 26:42 Again, for the second time, he went away and prayed, "My Father, if this cannot pass unless I drink it, thy will be done." 26:43 …again he came and found them sleeping, for their eyes were heavy. 26:44 So, leaving them again, he went away and prayed for the third time, saying the same words. 26:45 Then he came to the disciples… 14:41 …and said to them, "Are you still sleeping and taking your rest? It is enough; the hour has come; the Son of man is betrayed into the hands of sinners. 14:42 Rise, let us be going; see, my betrayer is at hand."

10   18:2 Now Judas, who betrayed him, also knew the place; for Jesus often met there with his disciples. 18:3 So Judas, procuring a band of soldiers and some officers from the chief priests and the Pharisees, went there with lanterns and torches and weapons. 14:44 Now the betrayer had given them a sign, saying, "The one I shall kiss is the man; seize him and lead him away under guard."

11   26:47 While *Jesus* was still speaking, Judas came… 22:47 …he drew near to Jesus to kiss him; 22:48 …Jesus said to him, "Judas, would you betray the Son of man with a kiss?" 18:4 …Jesus, knowing all that was to befall him, came forward and said to them, "Whom do you seek?" 18:5 They answered, "Jesus of Nazareth." Jesus said, "I am he." 18:6 When he said… *this* …they drew back. 18:7 Again he asked, "Whom do you seek?" And they said, "Jesus of Nazareth." 18:8 Jesus answered… *again* …"I told you that I am he; so, if you seek me, let

Matthew | Mark | Luke | John

these men go." 26:50 ...then they came up and laid hands on Jesus and seized him. 18:10 ...Simon Peter... 14:47 ...drew his sword, and struck the slave of the high priest,... *whose* 18:10 ...name was Malchus, 14:47 ...and cut off his ear. 22:51 But Jesus said, "No more of this!" And he touched his ear and healed him. 26:52 ...Jesus said to... *Peter* ..."Put your sword back into its place; for all who take the sword will perish by the sword. 26:53 Do you think that I cannot appeal to my Father, and he will at once send me more than twelve legions of angels? 26:54 But how then should the scriptures be fulfilled...?" 26:55 At that hour Jesus said to the crowds,... 14:48 ..."Have you come out as against a robber, with swords and clubs to capture me? 14:49 Day after day I was with you in the temple teaching, and you did not seize me.... 26:56 But all this has taken place, that the scriptures of the prophets might be fulfilled."...

12   26:57 Then those who had seized Jesus... ***took*** ...him to Ca'iaphas the high priest, where the scribes and the elders had gathered. 18:15 ...Peter followed Jesus, and so did another disciple. As this disciple was known to the high priest, he entered the court of the high priest along with Jesus, 18:16 while Peter stood outside at the door. So the other disciple went out and spoke to the maid who kept the door and brought Peter in. 18:17 The maid...said to Peter, 26:69 ..."You were with Jesus the Galilean." 26:70 But he denied it before them all, saying, "I do not know what you mean." 18:18 Now the servants and officers had made a charcoal fire, because it was cold, and

they were standing and warming themselves; Peter also was with them, standing and warming himself.

13   18:13 First they led... *Jesus* ...to Annas; for he was the father-in-law of Ca'iaphas, who was high priest that year. 18:14 It was Ca'iaphas who had given counsel to the Jews that it was expedient that one man should die for the people. 26:59 Now the chief priests and the whole council sought false testimony against Jesus that they might put him to death, 26:60 but they found none.... At last two came forward 26:61 and said,... 14:58 "We heard him say, 'I will destroy this temple that is made with hands, and in three days I will build another, not made with hands.'" 26:62 ...the high priest stood up and said, "Have you no answer to make? What is it that these men testify against you?" 14:61 But... *Jesus* ...was silent and made no answer. Again the high priest asked him, "Are you the Christ, the Son of the Blessed? 26:64 Jesus said to him, "You have said so. But I tell you, hereafter you will see the Son of man seated at the right hand of Power, and coming on the clouds of heaven." 26:65 Then the high priest tore his robes, and said,... 14:63 ..."Why do we still need witnesses? 14:64 You have heard his blasphemy. What is your decision?"... 26:66 ... they answered, "He deserves death." 14:65 And some began to spit on him, and to cover his face, and to strike him, saying to him, "Prophesy!" And the guards received him with blows.

14   18:19 The high priest then questioned Jesus about his disciples and his teaching. 18:20 Jesus answered him, "I have spoken openly to the world; I have always taught in synagogues and in the temple, where all Jews come

Matthew | Mark | Luke | John

together; I have said nothing secretly. 18:21 Why do you ask me? Ask those who have heard me,…they know what I said." 18:22 When he had said this, one of the officers standing by struck Jesus with his hand, saying, "Is that how you answer the high priest?" 18:23 Jesus… ***replied*** …"If I have spoken wrongly, bear witness to the wrong; but if I have spoken rightly, why do you strike me?" 18:24 Annas then sent him bound to Ca′iaphas the high priest.

15   ***As*** 18:25 …Peter was standing and warming himself. They said to him, "Are not you also one of his disciples?" He denied it and said, "I am not." 14:70 … after a little while… 18:26 One of the servants of the high priest, a kinsman of the man whose ear Peter had cut off, asked… 26:73 …"Certainly you are also one of them, for your accent betrays you." 26:74 Then he began to invoke a curse on himself and to swear, "I do not know the man."… 22:60 …and immediately, while he was still speaking, the cock crowed. 22:61 …the Lord turned and looked at Peter. And Peter remembered how he had said to him, "Before the cock crows today, you will deny me three times." 22:62 And…***Peter***… he went out and wept bitterly.

16   22:63 Now the men who were holding Jesus mocked him and beat him; 22:64 they also blindfolded him and asked him, "Prophesy! Who is it that struck you?" 22:65 And they spoke many other words against him, reviling him.

17   22:66 When day came, the assembly of the elders

of the people gathered together, both chief priests and scribes; and they led him away to their council, …they said *to Jesus*, 22:67 "If you are the Christ, tell us." But he said to them, "If I tell you, you will not believe; 22:68 and if I ask you, you will not answer. 22:69 But from now on the Son of man shall be seated at the right hand of the power of God." 22:70 And they all said, "Are you the Son of God, then?"… *Jesus replied*, …"You say that I am." 22:71 And they said, "What further testimony do we need? We have heard it ourselves from his own lips."

18   27:3 When Judas, his betrayer, saw that he was condemned, he repented and brought back the thirty pieces of silver to the chief priests and the elders, 27:4 saying, "I have sinned in betraying innocent blood." They said, "What is that to us? See to it yourself." 27:5 And throwing down the pieces of silver in the temple, he departed; and he went and hanged himself. 27:6 But the chief priests, taking the pieces of silver, said, "It is not lawful to put them into the treasury, since they are blood money." 27:7 So they took counsel, and bought with them the potter's field, to bury strangers in. 27:8 Therefore that field has been called the Field of Blood to this day. 27:9 Then was fulfilled what had been spoken by the prophet Jeremiah, saying, "And they took the thirty pieces of silver, the price of him on whom a price had been set by some of the sons of Israel, 27:10 and they gave them for the potter's field, as the Lord directed me."

19   18:28 Then they led Jesus from the house of Ca'iaphas to the praetorium… 15:1 …and delivered him to Pilate. 18:28 …It was early…*and* 15:3 …the chief priests… 18:28 …themselves did not enter the

Matthew | Mark | Luke | John

praetorium, so that they might not be defiled, but might eat the passover. 18:29 So Pilate went out to them and said, "What accusation do you bring against this man?" 18:30 They answered him, "If this man were not an evildoer, we would not have handed him over." 18:31 Pilate said to them, "Take him yourselves and judge him by your own law." The Jews said, "It is not lawful for us to put any man to death." 18:32 This was to fulfill the word which Jesus had spoken to show by what death he was to die.

20   18:33 Pilate entered the praetorium and called Jesus… 27:11 Now Jesus stood before the governor; and the governor asked him, "Are you the King of the Jews?", Jesus said… 18:34 …"Do you say this of your own accord, or did others say it to you about me?" 18:35 Pilate answered, "Am I a Jew? Your own nation and the chief priests have handed you over to me; what have you done?" 18:36 Jesus answered, "My kingship is not of this world; if my kingship were of this world, my servants would fight, that I might not be handed over to the Jews; but my kingship is not from the world." 18:37 Pilate said to him, "So you are a king?" Jesus answered, "You say that I am a king. For this I was born, and for this I have come into the world, to bear witness to the truth. Every one who is of the truth hears my voice." 18:38 Pilate said to him, "What is truth? 27:13 …"Do you not hear how many things they testify against you?" 15:5 But Jesus made no further answer….

21   18:38 After…this… 23:4 …Pilate… 18:38 …went

out to the Jews again... 23:4 and...said to the chief priests and the multitudes, "I find no crime in this man." 23:5 But they were urgent, saying, "He stirs up the people, teaching throughout all Judea, from Galilee even to this place." 23:6 When Pilate heard this, he asked whether the man was a Galilean. 23:7 And when he learned that he belonged to Herod's jurisdiction, he sent him over to Herod, who was himself in Jerusalem at that time. 23:8 When Herod saw Jesus, he was very glad, for he had long desired to see him...and he was hoping to see some sign done by him. 23:9 So he questioned him at some length; but... *Jesus* ...made no answer. 23:10 The chief priests and the scribes stood by, vehemently accusing him. 23:11 And Herod with his soldiers treated him with contempt and mocked him; then, arraying him in gorgeous apparel, he sent him back to Pilate. 23:12 ...Herod and Pilate became friends with each other that very day, for before this they had been at enmity with each other.

27:15 Now at the... 18:39 ...Passover... 27:15 ...feast the governor was accustomed to release for the crowd any one prisoner whom they wanted. 15:7 ...among the rebels in prison, who had committed murder in the insurrection, there was a man called Barab'bas. 23:13 Pilate then called together the chief priests and the rulers and the people, 23:14 and said to them, "You brought me this man as one who was perverting the people; and after examining him before you, behold, I did not find this man guilty of any of your charges against him; 23:15 neither did Herod, for he sent him back to us. Behold, nothing deserving death has been done by him;" 23:18 But they all cried out together, "Away with this

Matthew | Mark | Luke | John

man, and release to us Barab'bas". 15:12 ...Pilate again said to them, "Then what shall I do with the man whom you call the King of the Jews?" 15:13 And they cried out again, "Crucify him." 15:14 Pilate said, "Why, what evil has he done?" But they shouted all the more, "Crucify him."

23   19:6 Pilate said to them, "Take him yourselves and crucify him, for I find no crime in him." 19:7 The Jews answered him, "We have a law, and by that law he ought to die, because he has made himself the Son of God." 19:8 When Pilate heard these words, he was the more afraid; 19:9 he entered the praetorium again and said to Jesus, "Where are you from?" But Jesus gave no answer. 19:10 Pilate therefore said to him, "You will not speak to me? Do you not know that I have power to release you, and power to crucify you?" 19:11 Jesus answered, "You would have no power over me unless it had been given you from above; therefore he who delivered me to you has the greater sin."

24   19:12 Upon this Pilate sought to release him, but the Jews cried out, "If you release this man, you are not Caesar's friend; every one who makes himself a king sets himself against Caesar." 19:13 When Pilate heard these words, he brought Jesus out and sat down on the judgment seat at a place called The Pavement, and in Hebrew, Gab'batha. 27:19 ...while he was sitting on the judgment seat, his wife sent word to him, "Have nothing to do with that righteous man, for I have suffered much over him today in a dream."

25   19:14 Now it was the day of Preparation of the Passover; it was about the sixth hour. He said to the Jews, "Behold your King!" 19:15 They cried out, "Away with him, away with him, crucify him!"… 27:24 So when Pilate saw that he was gaining nothing, but rather that a riot was beginning, he took water and washed his hands before the crowd, saying, "I am innocent of this man's blood; see to it yourselves." 27:25 And all the people answered, "His blood be on us and on our children!" 27:26 Then he released for them Barab'bas, and having scourged Jesus, delivered him to be crucified.

26   15:16 …the soldiers led him away… 27:27 …into the praetorium, and they gathered the whole battalion before him. 27:28 …they stripped him and put a scarlet robe upon him, 27:29 and plaiting a crown of thorns they put it on his head, and put a reed in his right hand. … kneeling before him they mocked him, saying, "Hail, King of the Jews!" 15:18 And they began to salute him… 15:19 …they struck his head with a reed, and spat upon him, and they knelt down in homage to him. 27:31 …when they had mocked him, they stripped him of the robe, … put his own clothes on him, and led him away to crucify him.

27   N3 19:17 …they took Jesus, and he went out, bearing his own cross… 23:26 And as they led him away, they seized Simon of Cyre'ne,… 15:21 …the father of Alexander and Rufus… 27:32 …to carry his cross. 23:27 And there followed him a great multitude of the people, and of women who bewailed and lamented him. 23:28 But Jesus turning to them said, "Daughters of Jerusalem, do not weep for me, but weep for yourselves and for

Matthew | Mark | Luke | John

your children. 23:29 For behold, the days are coming when they will say, 'Blessed are the barren, and the wombs that never bore, and the breasts that never gave suck!' 23:30 Then they will begin to say to the mountains, 'Fall on us'; and to the hills, 'Cover us.' 23:31 For if they do this when the wood is green, what will happen when it is dry?"

28 23:32 Two others also, who were criminals, were led away to be put to death with… *Jesus*. 23:33 And when they came to the… 27:33 …place called Gol'gotha (which,… 19:17 …in Hebrew… 27:33 …means the place of a skull), 23:33 …they crucified him, and the criminals, one on the right and one on the left. 23:34 And Jesus said, "Father, forgive them; for they know not what they do."… 15:23 …they offered him wine mingled with myrrh; but he did not take it. 19:19 Pilate wrote a title and put it on the cross; it read, "Jesus of Nazareth, the King of the Jews." 19:20 Many of the Jews read this title, for the place where Jesus was crucified was near the city; and it was written in Hebrew, in Latin, and in Greek. 19:21 The chief priests of the Jews then said to Pilate, "Do not write, 'The King of the Jews,' but, 'This man said, I am King of the Jews.'" 19:22 Pilate answered, "What I have written I have written."

29 19:23 The soldiers took his garments and made four parts, one for each soldier; also his tunic. But the tunic was without seam, woven from top to bottom; 19:24 so they said to one another, "Let us not tear it, but cast lots for it to see whose it shall be." This was to fulfill the scripture, "They parted my garments among them, and for my clothing they cast lots."

30   23:35 The people stood by, watching; but the rulers scoffed at him, saying, "He saved others; let him save himself, if he is the Christ of God, his Chosen One!" 27:40 ...you who would destroy the temple and build it in three days, save yourself! If you are the Son of God, come down from the cross." 27:41 So also the chief priests, with the scribes and elders, mocked him, saying, 27:42 "He saved others; he cannot save himself.... 15:32 Let the Christ, the King of Israel, come down now from the cross, that we may see and believe."...

31   25:39 One of the criminals who were hanged railed at him, saying, "Are you not the Christ? Save yourself and us!" 25:40 But the other rebuked him, saying, "Do you not fear God, since you are under the same sentence of condemnation? 25:41 And we indeed justly; for we are receiving the due reward of our deeds; but this man has done nothing wrong." 25:42 And he... *continued*, ..."Jesus, remember me when you come into your kingdom." 25:43 *Jesus* ...said to him, "Truly, I say to you, today you will be with me in Paradise."

32   19:25 ....standing by the cross of Jesus were his mother, and his mother's sister, Mary the wife of Clopas, and Mary Mag'dalene. 19:26 When Jesus saw his mother and... *John*, ...the disciple whom he loved, standing near he said to his mother, "Woman, behold, your son!" 19:27 Then he said to the disciple, "Behold, your mother!" And from that hour the disciple took her to his own home.

33   15:34 ...at the ninth hour... 23:44 ...while the sun's light failed,... 15:34 ...Jesus cried with a loud voice,

Matthew | Mark | Luke | John

"E'lo-i, E'lo-i, la'ma sabach-tha'ni?" which means, "My God, my God, why hast thou forsaken me?" 15:35 And some of the bystanders hearing it said, "Behold, he is calling Eli'jah." 19:28 After this Jesus, knowing that all was now finished, said..., "I thirst." 19:29 A bowl full of vinegar stood there; so they put a sponge full of the vinegar on hyssop and held it to his mouth. 19:30 When Jesus had received the vinegar, he said, "It is finished"... 23:46 ... having said this... 19:30 ...he bowed his head... 23:46 ...breathed his last. 19:30 ...and gave up his spirit.

----

34   27:51 And behold, the curtain of the temple was torn in two, from top to bottom; and the earth shook, and the rocks were split; 27:52 the tombs also were opened, and many bodies of the saints who had fallen asleep were raised. 27:54 When the centurion and those who were with him, keeping watch over Jesus, saw the earthquake and what took place, they were filled with awe, and said, "Truly this was the Son of God!" 15:40 There were also women looking on from afar, among whom were Mary Mag'dalene, and Mary the mother of James the younger and of Joses, and Salo'me, 15:41 who, when he was in Galilee, followed him, and ministered to him; and also many other women who came up with him to Jerusalem.

35   19:31 Since it was the day of Preparation, in order to prevent the bodies from remaining on the cross on the

sabbath (for that sabbath was a high day), the Jews asked Pilate that their legs might be broken, and that they might be taken away. 19:32 So the soldiers came and broke the legs of the first, and of the other who had been crucified with him; 19:33 but when they came to Jesus and saw that he was already dead, they did not break his legs. 19:34 But one of the soldiers pierced his side with a spear, and at once there came out blood and water. 19:35 He who saw it has borne witness—his testimony is true, and he knows that he tells the truth—that you also may believe. 19:36 For these things took place that the scripture might be fulfilled, "Not a bone of him shall be broken." 19:37 And again another scripture says, "They shall look on him whom they have pierced."

36   27:57 When it was evening,… 15:43 Joseph of Arimathe′a, a respected member of the council, who was also himself looking for the kingdom of God, took courage and went to Pilate, and asked for the body of Jesus. 15:44 …Pilate wondered if he were already dead; and summoning the centurion, he asked him whether he was already dead. 15:45 …when he learned from the centurion that he was dead,… *Pilot* …granted the body to Joseph. 19:38 …so he came and took away his body. 19:39 Nicode′mus also, who had at first come to him by night, came bringing a mixture of myrrh and aloes, about a hundred pounds' weight. 19:40 They took the body of Jesus, and bound it in linen cloths with the spices, as is the burial custom of the Jews. 19:41 Now in the place where he was crucified there was a garden, and in the garden a new… 23:53 rock-hewn tomb 19:41 …where no one had ever been laid. 19:42 So because of the Jewish

Matthew | Mark | Luke | John

day of Preparation, as the tomb was close at hand, they laid Jesus there.

37   23:55 The women who had come with him from Galilee followed, and saw the tomb, and how his body was laid; 23:56 then they returned, and prepared spices and ointments. On the Sabbath they rested according to the commandment.

38   27:62 *The* Next day, that is, after the day of Preparation, the chief priests and the Pharisees gathered before Pilate 27:63 and said, "Sir, we remember how that imposter said, while he was still alive, 'After three days I will rise again.' 27:64 Therefore order the sepulcher to be made secure until the third day, lest his disciples go and steal him away, and tell the people, 'He has risen from the dead,' and the last fraud will be worse than the first." 27:65 Pilate said to them, "You have a guard of soldiers; go, make it as secure as you can." 27:66 So they went and made the sepulcher secure by sealing the stone and setting a guard.

39   16:1 And when the sabbath was past,... 28:1 ... toward the dawn of the first day of the week,... 16:1 ... Mary Mag'dalene, and Mary the mother of James, and Salo'me, bought spices, so that they might go and anoint him. 16:3 They were saying to one another, "Who will roll away the stone for us from the door of the tomb?" 28:2 And behold, there was a great earthquake; for an angel of the Lord descended from heaven and came, rolled back the stone, and sat upon it. 28:3 His appearance was like lightning, and his raiment white as

snow. 28:4 For fear of him the guards trembled and became like dead men. 24:3 But when... *the women* ... went in they did not find the body. 24:4 While they were perplexed about this... 28:5 ...the angel said to... *them*, 24:5 ..."Why do you seek the living among the dead? 24:6 Remember how he told you, while he was still in Galilee, 24:7 that the Son of man must be delivered into the hands of sinful men, and be crucified, and on the third day rise." 24:8 And they remembered his words. *The angel continued.* 28:5 ..."Do not be afraid;... 28:6 He is not here; for he has risen, as he said.... 28:7 ...go quickly... 16:7 ...tell his disciples and Peter that he is going before you to Galilee; there you will see him...." 28:8 So they departed quickly from the tomb with fear and great joy, and ran to tell his disciples.

40   20:3 Peter then came out with the other disciple, 20:2 the one whom Jesus loved, 20:3 and they went toward the tomb. 20:4 They both ran, but the other disciple outran Peter and reached the tomb first; 20:5 and stooping to look in, he saw the linen cloths lying there, but he did not go in. 20:6 Then...Peter came, following him, and went into the tomb; he saw the linen cloths lying, 20:7 and the napkin, which had been on his head, not lying with the linen cloths but rolled up in a place by itself. 20:8 Then the other disciple, who reached the tomb first, also went in, and he saw and believed; 20:9 for as yet they did not know the scripture, that he must rise from the dead. 20:10 Then the disciples went back to their homes.

41   20:11 *Now* ...Mary... *Mag'dalene* ...stood weeping outside the tomb, and as she wept she stooped

Matthew | Mark | Luke | John

to look into the tomb; *The* 20:12 ...angels in white, sitting where the body of Jesus had lain, one at the head and one at the feet. 20:13 ...said to her, "Woman, why are you weeping?" She said to them, "Because they have taken away my Lord, and I do not know where they have laid him." 20:14 Saying this, she turned round and saw Jesus standing, but she did not know that it was Jesus. 20:15 Jesus said to her, "Woman, why are you weeping? Whom do you seek?" Supposing him to be the gardener, she said to him, "Sir, if you have carried him away, tell me where you have laid him, and I will take him away." 20:16 Jesus said to her, "Mary." She turned and said to him in Hebrew, "Rab-bo′ni!" (which means Teacher). 20:17 Jesus said to her, "Do not hold me, for I have not yet ascended to the Father; but go to my brethren and say to them, I am ascending to my Father and your Father, to my God and your God." 20:18 Mary went and said to the disciples, "I have seen the Lord"; and she told them that he had said these things to her.

42   28:11 ...some of the guard went into the city and told the chief priests all that had taken place. 28:12 And when they had assembled with the elders and taken counsel, they gave a sum of money to the soldiers 28:13 and said, "Tell people, 'His disciples came by night and stole him away while we were asleep.' 28:14 And if this comes to the governor's ears, we will satisfy him and keep you out of trouble." 28:15 So they took the money and did as they were directed; and this story has been spread among the Jews to this day.

43   24:13 That very day two of... *Jesus' followers* ... were going to a village named Emma'us, about seven miles from Jerusalem, 24:14 and... *talked* ...with each other about all these things that had happened. 24:15 While they were talking and discussing together, Jesus himself drew near and went with them. 24:16 But their eyes were kept from recognizing him. 24:17 And he said to them, "What is this conversation which you are holding with each other as you walk?" And they stood still, looking sad.

44   24:18 Then one of them, named Cle'opas, answered him, "Are you the only visitor to Jerusalem who does not know the things that have happened there in these days?" 24:19 And he said to them, "What things?" ...*they replied*..., "Concerning Jesus of Nazareth, who was a prophet mighty in deed and word before God and all the people, 24:20 and how our chief priests and rulers delivered him up to be condemned to death, and crucified him. 24:21 But we had hoped that he was the one to redeem Israel. Yes, and besides all this, it is now the third day since this happened. 24:22 Moreover, some women of our company amazed us. They were at the tomb early in the morning 24:23 and did not find his body; and they came back saying that they had even seen a vision of angels, who said that he was alive. 24:24 Some of those who were with us went to the tomb, and found it just as the women had said; but him they did not see."

45   24:25 He said to them, "O foolish men, and slow of heart to believe all that the prophets have spoken! 24:26 Was it not necessary that the Christ should suffer these things and enter into his glory?" 24:27 And

Matthew | Mark | Luke | John

beginning with Moses and all the prophets, he interpreted to them in all the scriptures the things concerning himself.

46   24:28 So they drew near to the village to which they were going. He appeared to be going further, 24:29 but they constrained him, saying, "Stay with us, for it is toward evening and the day is now far spent." So he went in to stay with them. 24:30 When he was at table with them, he took the bread … blessed, and broke it, and gave it to them. 24:31 …their eyes were opened and… as … they recognized him;… he vanished out of their sight. 24:32 They said to each other, "Did not our hearts burn within us while he talked to us on the road, while he opened to us the scriptures?"

47   ***The two*** 24:33 …rose that same hour and returned to Jerusalem; and they found the eleven gathered together,… ***Even with*** 20:19 …the doors being shut…for fear of the Jews, Jesus came and stood among them and said to them, "Peace be with you." 20:20 When he had said this, he showed them his hands and his side. Then the disciples were glad when they saw the Lord. 20:21 Jesus said to them again, "Peace be with you. As the Father has sent me, even so I send you." 20:22 And when he had said this, he breathed on them, and said to them, "Receive the Holy Spirit. 20:23 If you forgive the sins of any, they are forgiven; if you retain the sins of any, they are retained."

48   20:24 Now Thomas, one of the twelve, called the Twin, was not with them when Jesus came. 20:25 So the

other disciples told him, "We have seen the Lord." But he said to them, "Unless I see in his hands the print of the nails, and place my finger in the mark of the nails, and place my hand in his side, I will not believe."

49   20:26 Eight days later, his disciples were again in the house, and Thomas was with them. The doors were shut, but Jesus came and stood among them, and said, "Peace be with you." 20:27 Then he said to Thomas, "Put your finger here, and see my hands; and put out your hand, and place it in my side; do not be faithless, but believing." 20:28 Thomas answered him, "My Lord and my God!" 20:29 Jesus said to him, "Have you believed because you have seen me? Blessed are those who have not seen and yet believe."

50   21:1 After this Jesus revealed himself again to the disciples by the Sea of Tibe′ri-as; and he revealed himself in this way. 21:2 Simon Peter, Thomas called the Twin, Nathan′a-el of Cana in Galilee, the sons of Zeb′edee, and two others of his disciples were together. 21:3 Simon Peter said to them, "I am going fishing." They said to him, "We will go with you." They went out and got into the boat; but that night they caught nothing.

51   21:4 Just as day was breaking, Jesus stood on the beach; yet the disciples did not know that it was Jesus. 21:5 Jesus said to them, "Children, have you any fish?" They answered him, "No." 21:6 He said to them, "Cast the net on the right side of the boat, and you will find some." So they cast it, and now they were not able to haul it in, for the quantity of fish. 21:7 That disciple whom Jesus loved said to Peter, "It is the Lord!" When Simon Peter heard that it was the Lord, he put on his

Matthew | Mark | Luke | **John**

clothes, for he was stripped for work, and sprang into the sea. 21:8 But the other disciples came in the boat, dragging the net full of fish, for they were not far from the land, but about a hundred yards off.

52   21:9 When they got out on land, they saw a charcoal fire there, with fish lying on it, and bread. 21:10 Jesus said to them, "Bring some of the fish that you have just caught." 21:11 So Simon Peter went aboard and hauled the net ashore, full of large fish, a hundred and fifty-three of them; and although there were so many, the net was not torn. 21:12 Jesus said to them, "Come and have breakfast." Now none of the disciples dared ask him, "Who are you?" They knew it was the Lord. 21:13 Jesus came and took the bread and gave it to them, and so with the fish. 21:14 This was now the third time that Jesus was revealed to the disciples after he was raised from the dead.

53   21:15 When they had finished breakfast, Jesus said to Simon Peter, "Simon, son of John, do you love me more than these?" He said to him, "Yes, Lord; you know that I love you." ***Jesus*** …said…, "Feed my lambs." 21:16 A second time he said to… ***Peter*** …,"Simon, son of John, do you love me?" He said to him, "Yes, Lord; you know that I love you." He said to him, "Tend my sheep." 21:17 ***Jesus*** …said … the third time, "Simon, son of John, do you love me?" Peter was grieved because he said to him the third time, "Do you love me?" And he said to him, "Lord, you know everything; you know that I love you." Jesus said to him, "Feed my sheep. 21:18 Truly, truly, I

say to you, when you were young, you girded yourself and walked where you would; but when you are old, you will stretch out your hands, and another will gird you and carry you where you do not wish to go." 21:19 (This he said to show by what death he was to glorify God.)…

54   16:15 *Then* …he said to them, "Go into all the world and preach the gospel to the whole creation. 16:16 He who believes and is baptized will be saved; but he who does not believe will be condemned. 16:17 And these signs will accompany those who believe: in my name they will cast out demons; they will speak in new tongues; 16:18 they will pick up serpents, and if they drink any deadly thing, it will not hurt them; they will lay their hands on the sick, and they will recover." 21:19 …And after this he said, "Follow me."

55   24:50 Then he led them out as far as Bethany, and lifting up his hands he blessed them. *Saying* 28:18 …"All authority in heaven and on earth has been given to me. 28:19 Go therefore and make disciples of all nations, baptizing them in the name of the Father and of the Son and of the Holy Spirit, 28:20 teaching them to observe all that I have commanded you;…

56   28:20 …I am with you always, to the close of the age."

57   24:51 While he blessed them, he parted from them, was carried up into heaven 16:19 …and sat down at the right hand of God.

Notes from the Reference Text

N1 – pg 34   Here you will notice that there is a significant jump in the verses from John as chapters 14-17 are omitted. These 4 chapters are a continuous dialog between Jesus and the disciples while around the Passover table and have no counterpart in the other Gospels. While this section is a treasure trove of lessons and stories from Jesus, and is a must read, it does not move the Passion story forward in the way the other Gospels do at this point.

N2 – pg 34   Luke 22:43-44. Many early manuscripts of scripture do not have these two verses and they are not included in the RSV translation except as footnotes. I inserted these verses into place for this book.

N3 – pg 43   The stations of the cross, as traditionally known, include stations that have a direct biblical source (1, 2, 5, 8, 10-14) and stations that do not (3, 4, 6, 7, and 9.) As a result, there may be some details that appear to have been omitted in this book.

For example, the fifth traditional station tells of when Simon of Cyrene is called on to carry the cross for Jesus. This event has a direct source in the Gospels and can be found in MT 27:32, MK 15:21, and LK 23:26. Yet there is no reference, in any of the Gospels, to Jesus' three falls (traditional stations 3, 7, and 9.)

In 1991 Pope John Paul II introduced The Scriptural Way of the Cross based more closely on the details described in the Passion accounts. In 2007, Pope Benedict XVI supported this set of stations as an alternate to the traditional stations for use during meditation and public celebration.

The Traditional Stations of the Cross
1. Pilate condemns Jesus to die
2. Jesus accepts his cross
3. Jesus falls for the first time
4. Jesus meets his mother, Mary
5. Simon of Cyrene helps carry the cross
6. Veronica wipes the face of Jesus
7. Jesus falls for the second time
8. Jesus meets the women of Jerusalem
9. Jesus falls for the third time
10. Jesus is stripped of his clothes
11. Jesus is nailed to the cross
12. Jesus dies on the cross
13. Jesus is taken down from the cross
14. Jesus is placed in the tomb

The Scriptural Way of the Cross
1. Jesus in the Garden of Gethsemane
2. Jesus is betrayed by Judas and arrested
3. Jesus is condemned by the Sanhedrin
4. Jesus is denied by Peter
5. Jesus is judged by Pilate
6. Jesus is scourged and crowned with thorns
7. Jesus takes up his cross
8. Jesus is helped by Simon of Cyrene to carry his cross
9. Jesus meets the women of Jerusalem
10. Jesus is crucified
11. Jesus promises his kingdom to the repentant thief
12. Jesus entrusts Mary and John to each other
13. Jesus dies on the cross
14. Jesus is laid in the tomb

Lightning Source UK Ltd.
Milton Keynes UK
UKHW051844110220
358544UK00009B/133